THE SOLAR SYSTEM

A TRUE BOOK

by

Paul P. Sipiera

Children's Press®

A Division of Grolier Publishing

New York London Hong Kong Sydney
Danbury, Connecticut

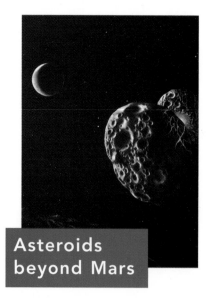

Asteroids
beyond Mars

Reading Consultant
Linda Cornwell
Learning Resource Consultant
Indiana Department of
Education

Science Consultant
Samuel Storch
Lecturer,
American Museum-Hayden
Planetarium, New York City

Dedication: To my wife,
Diane, and our daughters,
Andrea, Paula Frances,
and Carrie Ann

Library of Congress Cataloging-in-Publication Data

Sipiera, Paul P.
    The solar system / by Paul Sipiera.
       p.   cm. — (A true book)
    Includes bibliographical references and index.
    Summary: Describes the sun, the planets, and the asteroids that make up our solar system.
    ISBN 0-516-20339-8 (lib.bdg.)   0-516-26175-4 (pbk.)
    1. Solar System—Juvenile literature. [1. Solar System.]
I. Title. II. Series.
QB501.3.S64 1997
523.2—dc20
                                                            96-28556
                                                                 CIP
                                                                 AC

         15 R 06

Contents

Pluto

Neptune

Uranus

Saturn

Jupiter

Earth

Mars

Mercury

Venus

The solar system

The Origin of the Solar System

The solar system consists of an average-sized star, called the Sun, and a family of nine planets. All the planets orbit, or circle, the Sun. Some of these planets, like Earth, are small and rocky worlds. Others are large and made up mostly of frozen gases.

EUROPA

TRITON

IO

MOON

GANYMEDE

CALLISTO

TITAN

Smaller objects called moons orbit many of the planets. Moons come in different sizes and are made of different materials. At the outer edge of the solar system, farthest from the Sun, lies a cloud of comets.

The solar system began nearly five billion years ago with the formation of the Sun. Stars like our Sun were made from the collapse of a large cloud of gas and dust called a nebula. This collapse was caused by the force of gravity pulling things together.

An artist's impression of a star-forming nebula

As this gas cloud became smaller, it began to get hotter in the center. In time, the infant Sun began to glow. Surrounding this glowing ball was a haze of gas, dust, and ice. This material formed the planets.

Just as gravity pulled huge amounts of gas together to form the Sun, gravity did the same for the planets. The amount of matter pulled together helped decide whether a planet would be rocky or made of gas. Nearest

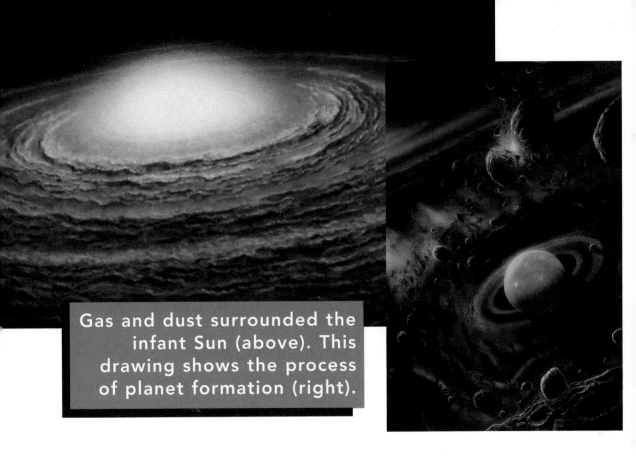

Gas and dust surrounded the infant Sun (above). This drawing shows the process of planet formation (right).

the Sun, the temperatures were hottest. Only planets made of rock and metal could form there. Far from the Sun, temperatures were much cooler. Here, planets made of gas were more likely to form.

A Family of Planets

The planets of our solar system all revolve around the Sun, but at various distances from it. The force of the Sun's gravity pulls the planets along in their orbits. The planets, in turn, pull back on the Sun. Both forces are equal to each other. This prevents the planets from falling into the Sun. The same is true for moons orbiting planets.

The force of gravity differs from planet to planet. It depends on the planet's mass. A planet with a low mass, like Mars, has a weak gravity. Massive planets, like Jupiter, have a strong gravity.

Closest to the Sun are Mercury, Venus, Earth, and Mars. These four are known as the Earth-like planets. Like

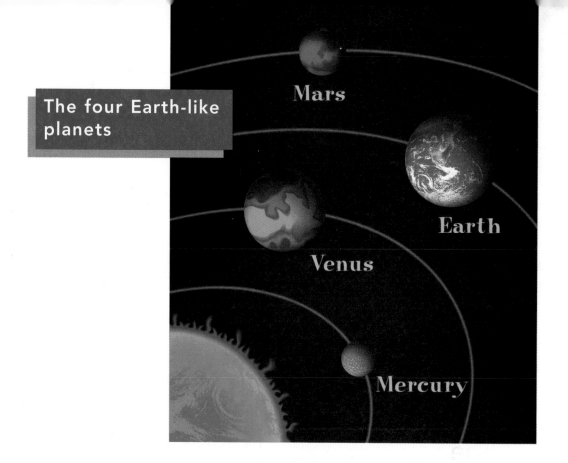

Mars

Earth

Venus

Mercury

the Earth, they are small, solid, and made of rock and metal.

Beyond Mars lie the "gas giants"—Jupiter, Saturn, Uranus, and Neptune. These four are known as the Jupiter-like planets.

Saturn

Uranus

Earth

Neptune

Jupiter

A drawing showing how the four "gas giants" compare in size to Earth

They are huge and made of gas. Each planet has a large family of moons, and a system of rings.

Beyond the gas giants lies little Pluto. Pluto is unlike any other planet. It looks more like one of the moons of the gas planets.

Mercury and Venus

Mercury is the planet nearest the Sun. It is about one-third the size of Earth, and has no atmosphere to protect its surface from the Sun's heat. In sunlight, the temperature can climb to over 806° Fahrenheit (430° Celsius). In shadow, the temperature can fall below

Mercury, as seen from the *Mariner 9* spacecraft (left), and the cratered surface of Mercury (right)

-279°F (-173°C). This happens because Mercury has no atmosphere to balance its temperature. It is always either very hot or very cold.

The surface of Mercury is covered with craters. These

craters were made by meteoroids hitting the planet's surface. A planet with an atmosphere, like Earth, has few craters. This is because the atmosphere causes all but the biggest meteoroids to burn up before hitting the ground. Because Mercury has no atmosphere, all the meteoroids get through, hitting the planet at very high speeds.

The next planet beyond Mercury is Venus. It is often

The planet
Venus

called Earth's twin because of
its similar size. Like Earth,
Venus is covered by clouds, but
the clouds of Venus are very
different. They are made not of
water, like Earth's clouds, but
of tiny sulfur crystals and
droplets of sulfuric acid.

Venus's atmosphere is also different from Earth's. It is made of carbon dioxide, the gas that makes bubbles in soda pop. Venus's atmosphere traps heat from the Sun, so that Venus's surface temperature can reach 882°F (472°C). This is called the "greenhouse effect." Such high temperatures make it unlikely for life to exist on Venus.

Earth and Its Moon

The third planet from the Sun is Earth. It takes one year for Earth to orbit the Sun. Earth is a water-covered planet unlike any other. Its atmosphere is oxygen-rich. Seen from space, Earth is very beautiful. Its blue seas, rusty-red continents, white clouds, and polar ice

caps all make it a colorful planet. It seems that Earth is an ideal place for life to exist. Earth is orbited by one moon. It takes one month for the Moon to orbit Earth. The

Earth's Moon (left), and a drawing of a crater being formed on the Moon (above)

Moon looks like Mercury—it is covered with craters and has no atmosphere. In daylight, the temperature can rise to 266°F (130°C). At night it falls to -274°F (-170°C).

Mars

The last of the small, rocky worlds is Mars. Mars is called the "Red Planet" because its surface is covered by rusty-red dust. It has many of Earth's features—dry river valleys, long canyons, old volcanoes, and polar ice caps. Two tiny moons, Phobos and Deimos, orbit the planet.

The planet Mars (left) has a surface covered with rusty-red dust (below).

Mars is slightly more than half the size of Earth. Like Earth, it has four seasons, but they are twice as long, and much colder.

Phobos and Deimos, the two small moons of Mars

The atmosphere of Mars is made up of carbon dioxide, is very thin, and does not hold heat well. In summer, the temperature may reach 68°F (20°C) during the day. At night, the temperature is cold enough to freeze carbon dioxide into snow.

The Asteroid Belt

Between the orbits of Mars and Jupiter lies a region called the asteroid belt. Here, thousands of bodies of rock and metal of all sizes can be found. The largest is called Ceres. It has a diameter of 600 miles (1,000 kilometers). It was once thought to be a

An artist's impression
of the asteroid belt

planet. All other asteroids are
smaller. Scientists believe the
asteroids are all that is left of
material that never formed
into planets.

Jupiter and Saturn

Beyond the asteroid belt orbits Jupiter. This giant planet is 11 times bigger than Earth and is made of hydrogen gas. When we look at Jupiter, we see only its cloud tops. The clouds of Jupiter appear in different colors when viewed through a telescope.

The clouds of Jupiter (right) and Jupiter's Great Red Spot (above)

Huge "storms" can also be seen. One of these is called the Great Red Spot. It is about three times as large as the Earth!

Jupiter's Great Red Spot

The word "volume" is used to describe how much space an object takes up. Jupiter has the largest volume of all the planets. About 1,394 Earths could easily fit inside it! **Jupiter's Great Red Spot alone could fit three Earths across it!**

A thin ring of ice and dust surrounds Jupiter. Jupiter has a family of sixteen moons. One of these moons, Io, has erupting volcanoes on it. Another moon, Europa, may be covered by a frozen ocean.

This view of Io (below) shows a volcano erupting on the horizon. Cracks are visible in the ice of Europa (right).

A color-enhanced photo of Saturn

Saturn is one of the most beautiful objects that can be seen through a telescope. It has a wonderful system of rings surrounding its yellowish ball.

These rings are made of small chunks of ice and rock. The rings are very wide, but thin. They are easily seen because they reflect light so well.

Saturn is made mostly of hydrogen and helium, which are very light gases. Because of this, the planet is not very dense. If we could put Saturn in a tub of water large enough to hold it, the planet would float like a cork!

A drawing of Saturn and several of its moons

So far, scientists have identified 18 moons orbiting Saturn. There may be more. One moon, Titan, has an atmosphere that is thicker than Earth's.

Uranus and Neptune

Most of the planets rotate around an imaginary axis. This can be demonstrated by spinning a globe you might have in your classroom. When compared to the Sun, the Earth's axis appears to be tilted by 23.5 degrees. This tilt is the cause of seasons.

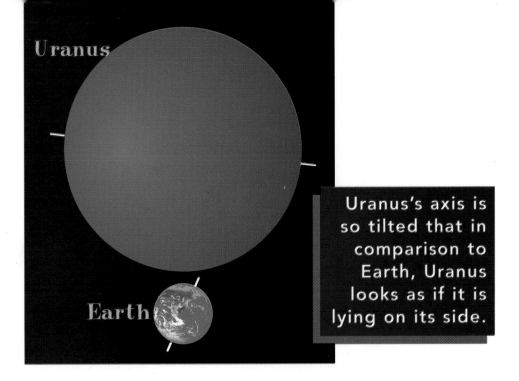

Uranus

Earth

Uranus's axis is so tilted that in comparison to Earth, Uranus looks as if it is lying on its side.

The planet Uranus is tilted 98 degrees on its axis. Because of this, its seasons are the most extreme of any planet in the solar system. On Uranus, the equator is always cold, and one pole or the other always points to the Sun.

Like Saturn and Jupiter, Uranus has rings. But the rings of Uranus are thin and dark, making them hard to see. Fifteen small ice moons orbit Uranus. A moon called Miranda looks like it broke apart and later came back together again! This is most unusual.

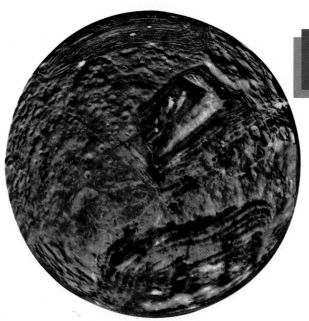

Miranda, one of Uranus's moons

The planet Neptune (left) and Neptune's giant dark spot (right)

The last of the gas giants is beautiful, blue Neptune. This planet has several rings and eight moons. As with the other gas planets, we see only its cloud tops. In 1989, the *Voyager* spacecraft discovered a great dark spot the size of

Earth in the clouds of Neptune. It later disappeared. Now a new spot has taken its place.

The rings of Neptune are unlike those of any other planet. They seem to be incomplete. Some areas are thick with particles, while others seem to have none. Scientists are not sure what this means.

One of Neptune's moons, called Triton, may have geysers erupting from its surface. These are not watery geysers, like

those found here on Earth, but rather eruptions of methane gas. Some astronomers believe that the planet Pluto may look like Triton.

Pluto and Beyond

Pluto is a small icy world that orbits the Sun differently from any other planet. Most planets orbit the Sun in nearly circular paths. Pluto's orbit is more oval-shaped and even comes inside Neptune's orbit, where it is now. In a few years, it is expected to return to its normal position.

In 1979, astronomers discovered that Pluto had a moon about one-half its size. That moon was named Charon. Since then, much has been learned about Pluto by observing the motion of Charon. Some scientists think that Pluto has more in common with Neptune's moon Triton than any planet.

Far, far beyond Pluto lies the edge of the solar system. It is called the Oort comet cloud. Comets are believed to come from here. Comets are small objects made of ice and rock. Scientists believe that they may be leftover material from the for-mation of the planets. Although Pluto is very far from the Sun, the Oort cloud is nearly 1,300 times farther away!

There may be millions of comets slowly orbiting the Sun. Perhaps all stars have an Oort cloud of comets surrounding them. Beyond that, there is only empty space between the stars—as far as we know!

To Find Out More

Here are some additional resources to help you learn more about the solar system:

 **Books**

Burrows, William E., **Mission to Deep Space: Voyagers' Journey of Discovery.** W.H. Freeman and Company, 1993.

Cole, Joanna, **The Magic School Bus Lost in the Solar System.** Scholastic, 1990.

Curtis, Anthony R., ed., **Space Almanac.** Gulf Publishing Company, 1992.

Gouch, Maura, **The Solar System.** Child's World, 1993.

Henbest, Nigel, **The Planets: A Guided Tour to the Solar System Through the Eyes of America's Space Probes.** Viking, 1992.

Leedy, Loreen, **Postcards from Pluto: A Tour of the Solar System.** Holiday House, 1993.

Muirden, James, **Stars and Planets.** Grolier, 1994.

Simon, Seymour, **Our Solar System.** Morrow Junior Books, 1992.

Organizations

Astronomical Society of the Pacific
1290 24th Avenue
San Francisco, CA 94122
http://www.physics.sfsu. edu/asp

Junior Astronomical Society
58 Vaughan Gardens
Ilford Essex IG1 3PD
England

The Planetary Society
5 North Catalina Avenue
Pasadena, CA 91106
e-mail: *tps.lc@genie.geis. com*

Online Sites

An Overview of the Solar System
http://isr.co.jp/tnp/overview. html

Exploring Our Solar System—and Beyond
http://www.reston.com/astro /explore.html

The Planetary Studies Foundation
http://homepage.interaccess. com/~jpatpsf/>.

Important Words

atmosphere the gases surrounding the Earth and some other planets

comet object made of ice, gas, and dust that has a long, glowing tail when near the Sun

geyser an explosion of steam or gas from the ground

gravity the force of attraction between two objects

matter substance that is either solid, liquid, or gas

meteoroid small particle of matter in the solar system

moon natural satellite that orbits a planet

planet large body that orbits a star, as Earth orbits the Sun; unlike stars, planets do not give off light

Index

Meet the Author

Paul P. Sipiera is a professor of geology and astronomy at William Rainey Harper College in Palatine, Illinois. His main area of research is meteorites. When he is not studying science, he can be found working on his farm in Galena, Illinois, with his wife, Diane, and their three daughters, Andrea, Paula Frances, and Carrie Ann.